Dear Mommy,

A Letter from Heaven

Alaina Smith

A super big hug and thank-you to my Lord and Savior, Jesus Christ, who has worked all things together for my good. To everyone, especially all my kids, who made this book possible. Thank you to my husband, for telling me I wrote something special, when the first few pages were done. For also continuously reminding me that great things take time. A special thank-you to my pastor, Steve Stienmetz, and his wife, Sharon. For your love, compassion, counsel, and help with so much in my life. Faith Kochanowski. Mari Peterson. Jim and Leslie Smith, for your help bringing it all together. Also my editor, and biggest support, Kelsey Bryant. You're truly a gem.

A thank-you especially to all the women who have given me a reason to publish it. You're overcomers, survivors, and brave.

Dear Mommy,

A Letter from Heaven

Alaina Smith

Dear Mommy,

You may be struggling a lot with so many thoughts now that I'm not with you, but guess what, Mommy?

I'm in Heaven.

Mommy,
no one here wears glasses or has tummy aches. I don't need to be scared of doctors or icky medicine. I never have bad dreams either! I never, EVER cry and I can't get hurt.

"He will wipe every tear from their eyes. There will be no more death or mourning or crying or pain, for the old order of things has passed away."

Revelation 21:4 NIV

I have no more tears or pain. I play A LOT, and do all sorts of awesome things with other kids. There are so many kids for me to play with. I'm never lonely. When you feel lonely or you're missing me, please talk to God about it, Mommy.

"God is our refuge and strength, always ready to help in times of trouble."

Psalm 46:1 NLT

There is no sin here, Mommy. Nothing bad ever happens here, and no one hurts anyone else. Mommy, everyone is so nice here! I'm always safe and it's never dark. I'm surrounded by love and beauty all the time!

"No longer will you need the sun to shine by day, nor the moon to give its light by night, for the Lord your God will be your everlasting light, and your God will be your glory. Your sun will never set; your moon will not go down. For the Lord will be your everlasting light. Your days of mourning will come to an end."
-Isaiah 60:19-20 NLT

Mommy,

Jesus takes wonderful care of me. So does everyone else. I cannot WAIT to show you everything some-day and have you meet so many people! And see angels! The angels are really, really neat, Mommy. They do so much for God.

"All heaven will praise your great wonders, Lord; myriads of angels will praise you for your faithfulness."

-Psalm 89:5 NLT

It's hard for others to understand what you're going through. Even other mommies who hurt inside still don't know because there's only one you. -It'll be okay, Mommy. God saw and knew you were going to hurt.

"The Lord is close to the broken-hearted; He rescues those whose spirits are crushed."

-Psalm 34:18 NLT

The world is broken and Jesus never promised it would be easy. Please don't doubt God, Mommy, or His power. He's really, really big. You gotta trust me. He's GINORMOUS, and our heavenly Father is wise and very good.

"…I saw the Lord sitting upon a throne, high and lifted up; and the train of His robe filled the temple."

-Isaiah 6:1b ESV

All I know is pure, undefiled love.
Please push to trust God, Mommy.
He cares for you. He can help you
feel better.
I can't stop smiling! It's all I do!

"Blessed be the God and Father of our Lord Jesus Christ, the Father of mercies and God of all comfort, who comforts us in all our affliction, so that we may be able to comfort those who are in any affliction, with the comfort with which we ourselves are comforted by God."

-2 Corinthians 1:3-4 ESV

I love you, Mommy. Lots and lots.
Jesus loves you so much, too.
Love,
Me
X o x o x o x o x o x o X o

"Even so it is not the will of your Father who is in heaven that one of these little ones should perish."

-Jesus in Matthew 18:14 NKJV

"I have told you these things, so that in me you may have peace. In this world you will have trouble. But take heart! I have overcome the world."

-Jesus in John 16:33 NIV

Letters from the Author

For the Mother with Regret:

Dear Mommy,

The Bible is clear that once we have faith in Jesus, trust Him, and go to Him for forgiveness, He's quick to forgive and He remembers our sins no more (Hebrews 8:12). What a miracle that is! But let's go a little deeper. How can the God of everything forget? It's not that He forgets, but rather it's like Jesus is our makeup...except better because His blood and sacrifice covers and washes away all the blemishes of sin. That is what the Lord sees when He looks at us. Jesus makes us beautiful and united with Him. And the most exciting part? His results stay with us..."Who then is the one who condemns? No one. Christ Jesus who died—more than that, who was raised to life—is at the right hand of God and is also interceding for us." -Romans 8:34 NIV

The problem may often be forgetting, because your body held life. You're bonded to that child, so what do you do now that you've lost a baby due to choices? How can a mommy possibly forget? The moment may be on repeat in your head and it's causing you deep, deep sorrow. You may even find yourself doing okay for a while; then you're blindsided by memories, and maybe the feelings of anger and regret happen all over again. If a man or someone else helped lead you to your sin, please forgive them and pray for them. People often have fear or deception in their hearts for many reasons. Jeremiah 17:9 ESV says, "The heart is deceitful above all things, and desperately sick; who can understand it?" Verse 10 then shows us who is in charge of all decisions of judgment and who to go to with your hurt.

"I the Lord search the heart and test the mind, to give every man according to his ways, according to the fruit of his deeds." It's God saying, "If you were wronged, I know all the reasons to both sides of the story, and I got your back." You can trust Him. It's not excusing what was done, but it's freeing you from the resentment and bitterness. Let the Lord handle their sin. If you've asked Him to forgive you, hold tight to the promise that you are indeed forgiven, and deeply loved.

In my experience as a Christian, there is nothing comparable to the love of Christ, which is absolutely perfect. He not only died for us but uses events in our lives to draw us to Himself. "For the kind of sorrow God wants us to experience leads us away from sin and results in salvation. There's no regret for that kind of sorrow. But worldly sorrow, which lacks repentance, results in spiritual death (2 Corinthians 7:10 NLT). Mommy, focus on the love Christ has for you, not the past failure of not trusting God. Focus on the absolute miraculous awesomeness that God made Heaven and made reunions possible for those trusting Him as Lord and Savior, despite their wrongs. If you have confided in people after the fact who judged you for your choices rather than pour love on you, I am so sorry. If you find you continue to judge yourself, give yourself permission to let go. Jesus' sacrifice is more than enough. Satan loves to have us remember; our adversary knows how to hurt us and do it well, so please focus on Christ and the reunion. What's done is done, but take joy in knowing that as long as you still have breath and you trust in Him, He's not done doing a great work in you.

For the Mother with Bitterness:

Dear Mommy,

It's not your fault, but like a Mother with Regret, your memories may be on repeat. Something tragic happened, whether it was a horrendous act, accident, or illness. Helplessness over not being able to change it gives way to anger, and bitterness threatens to squeeze life from your life. Your child is now safe and secure in the arms of the Savior and it doesn't take the void away, but the Lord is with you, and the Lord will deal with the wrongs accordingly. Why didn't God stop it? Why was this allowed? I don't have the answers, but I do know the Lord is sovereign. Maybe this is meant for an unexpected opportunity. Jesus not only chose to stay on His cross, but He also kept the other two men on their crosses. Jesus said that He was sent to do the will of Him who sent Him. God didn't tell Jesus to help them physically, but what transpired? One of the men experienced the miracle of his heart being accepted through forgiveness, and he had reassurance of salvation. Even though he would still suffer and die that day, he was going to leave this world and enter His rest.

"Then one of the criminals who were hanged blasphemed Him, saying, 'If You are the Christ, save Yourself and us.' But the other, answering, rebuked him, saying, 'Do you not even fear God, seeing you are under the same condemnation? And we indeed justly, for we receive the due reward of our deeds; but this Man has done nothing wrong.'

Then he said to Jesus, 'Lord, remember me when You come into Your kingdom.' And Jesus said to him, 'Assuredly, I say to you, today you will be with Me in Paradise.'" -Luke 23:39-43 NKJV

Jesus said in Matthew 18:14 NKJV, "Even so it is not the will of your Father who is in heaven that one of these little ones should perish."

Even though your little one isn't physically here, and the way they died wasn't what anyone should have to experience, you can rest easy knowing that he or she is with Jesus this day. This could be an opportunity for you to cling to Jesus and the cross in a way you never have before. I want to encourage you to go to the Lord and His wonderful personal love letters from heaven, which is His Word, with your hurt and not to other gods (such as drinking, drugs, eating problems, work, etc.). I ask that you show courage by driving your pain to Christ, and have Him sort through the layers of grief.

Jesus experienced the death of His stepfather and the death of His cousin, and He felt immense sorrow when Lazarus died. He felt tremendous sorrow and pain on the cross. He knows death and pain on levels we know only a little about, so, Mommy, cling to Him. He will give you rest and comfort that Satan wishes so much to keep stealing from you.

The void and the heaviness will still sometimes be there, but take heart in knowing you can find peace, joy, and rest in a wonderful Shepherd, and comfort in His Word.

For All the Grieving Mothers:

Dear Mommy,

This book is for the loss of a young child at any time, for any reason—miscarriage, trauma, sickness, and all other ways the world takes loved ones away. Either before they breathed their first breath and saw your face or after. You have an incredible opportunity now to allow this heartache in your life to bring you closer to the Father and to Jesus. My prayer for you is that you'll allow your experiences to drive you closer to the One who is relatable, to the One who knows what it is like to lose and suffer, and find Him through His Word. He suffered and died for all of us, whether we accept Him or not. Know that there's a Father who loves you with unconditional love and desires to be like a husband to you, except one who always desires all of you—heart, soul, mind, and strength—all the time. For the Mommy with Regret, this is very important for you to understand because if someone led you to your choices, you might suffer with feelings of rejection for many reasons. I have this to say: Jesus wants you. It's hard when we don't have a direct reason for the whys and for the pain other than sin entered the world through Adam and Eve's choices. Once sin entered in so did death, but you have hope in pain and trials, that they're an opportunity for great joy (James 1:2-3).

"Knowing that the testing of your faith produces patience. But let patience have its perfect work, that you may be perfect and complete, lacking nothing."
-James 1:3-4 NKJV

You now have a hope for a beautiful reunion with your little one. What a miracle and joy that is! I pray that this book helped you find the Lord in an unexpected way. If you never talked to Him before or have struggled, you can pray something like this:

Lord Jesus, please forgive me. I know I am a sinner. I know and believe You are Lord. I know you died for me and rose again, and that my little one is in Heaven with You, safe and sound. I ask that You come into my life and lead me with Your Holy Spirit. I surrender all I am to You. Thank you for Your love and sacrifice. Help me now to live for You, to have courage to take up my cross daily, and to be like You. In Jesus' name. Amen.

My dear Mommy, let's focus on the reunion every day, and remember I'm walking in this with you. Let's search the Scriptures daily, and know that our Savior, who not only died but rose again and is seated at the right hand of the Father, is also praying for us and walking with us.

All my love in Christ,
Alaina

Author's Note

What this book is and what it isn't.

I started this book in 2017, a few days after my second natural miscarriage, both of which happened between my second and third child. Before I was married, I bought into the birth control lies and the Google definition of the Plan B pill, memories I now trust Jesus with on a daily basis. This book is meant to be a tool to assist the grieving mom. To put in her hands a quick reference go-to for her pain. It's not to replace the Bible or sound counsel. It can save her from paging through the Bible over and over again for verses to help, because when a person is crying or mad, it's very hard to think straight and try to look through Scripture. I also took into consideration that maybe if she's not familiar with the Word, finding Scripture relatable would be extremely difficult. It is what I believe Heaven to be through a child's eyes, who only has a certain amount of time to write a quick letter to Mommy, to let her know they're okay, before they're off to play again.

There is so much about Heaven we simply don't know. We don't know how old anyone is in Heaven, or what age they're allowed to grow up into, if that even happens. The Bible isn't specific on this at all, which shouldn't be viewed negatively but rather as a major surprise party. I have portrayed this through a child's perspective, to illustrate some very special truths. Since we can't call our kids—or even hear the Lord's audible voice say, "They're doing so well!"—this is to act as that phone call.

I read a book about a child's possible experience with Heaven before and after I had my miscarriages. I thought about how all miscarried babies are in Heaven, how all aborted babies are in Heaven and probably more kids than we realize are in Heaven, and I thought about all the pain other women have experienced. I thought about all the women fighting the whys and lost in sorrow. I imagined my kids playing in Heaven and having not a care in the world. I asked myself, "What would my kids want me to know?" Then it went farther, "What would other kids want their mommy to know?" "What does the Lord want them to know?" Then I asked, "Lord, how can You use all my pain for Your glory?"

Then I wrote down the simple words, Dear Mommy.

This book is a gift, written from past and present heartache, in the hopes and prayers it can bring unexpected comfort to others, and help someone who is struggling meet their Savior.

Sincerely,
Alaina Smith

WestBow Press books may be ordered through booksellers or by contacting:

WestBow Press
A Division of Thomas Nelson & Zondervan
1663 Liberty Drive
Bloomington, IN 47403
www.westbowpress.com
844-714-3454

Because of the dynamic nature of the Internet, any web addresses or links contained in this book may have changed since publication and may no longer be valid. The views expressed in this work are solely those of the author and do not necessarily reflect the views of the publisher, and the publisher hereby disclaims any responsibility for them.

Scripture quotations marked (NIV) are taken from the Holy Bible, New International Version®, NIV®. Copyright © 1973, 1978, 1984, 2011 by Biblica, Inc.® Used by permission of Zondervan. All rights reserved worldwide. www.zondervan.com The "NIV" and "New International Version" are trademarks registered in the United States Patent and Trademark Office by Biblica, Inc.®

Scripture quotations marked (NLT) are taken from the Holy Bible, New Living Translation, copyright ©1996, 2004, 2015 by Tyndale House Foundation. Used by permission of Tyndale House Publishers, Carol Stream, Illinois 60188. All rights reserved.

Scripture quotations marked (ESV) are from the ESV® Bible (The Holy Bible, English Standard Version®), Copyright © 2001 by Crossway, a publishing ministry of Good News Publishers. Used by permission. All rights reserved.

Scripture marked (NKJV) taken from the New King James Version®. Copyright © 1982 by Thomas Nelson. Used by permission. All rights reserved.

ISBN: 978-1-6642-6651-3 (sc)
ISBN: 978-1-6642-6652-0 (e)

Library of Congress Control Number: 2022908804

WestBow Press rev. date: 11/02/2022

WESTBOW
P R E S S®
A DIVISION OF THOMAS NELSON
& ZONDERVAN